2014/2015

TH...

SCOTTISH NATIONALITY TEST

"HOW SCOTTISH ARE YOU?"

THE 2014 REFERENDUM EDITION

CAMERON McPHAIL

First published 2014
by Black & White Publishing Ltd
29 Ocean Drive, Edinburgh EH6 6JL

1 3 5 7 9 10 8 6 4 2   14 15 16 17

ISBN: 978 1 84502 780 3

Illustrations by Oli Nightingale of Kartoon Factory

Typeset by Creative Link, North Berwick
Printed and bound by Hussarbooks, Poland, www.hussarbooks.pl

CONTENTS

Introduction and Test Guidelines

Appendices

The 2014 Scottish Nationality Test
Embra, near Glasgow

Dear Candidate

SCOTLAND'S DATE WITH DESTINY: 18th SEPTEMBER 2014

This test does not seek to take sides. It merely indicates whether you are Scottish enough to consider voting in the Independence Referendum scheduled for 18th September.

The Nationality Test has been designed by some of Scotland's greatest thinkers on all matters Scottish. Towering academics from our greatest educational institutions have collaborated to compile a broad-based and balanced examination. The test is not designed to measure academic ability; rather, it reaches down into your soul and gauges the essence of your Scottishness. Take the Scottish Nationality Test and discover just how Scottish you are and whether you should even consider exercising your vote on the 18th.

This pack also includes the following three information sheets designed to help you make your mind up on how to vote on the day:

- An advance copy of the Referendum ballot paper (see page 4) so that you can consider both sides of the argument before 18th September. Please bear in mind that there is nothing wrong with selecting the 'mibbi aye, mibbi naw' option as your choice.

- In an effort to preserve the Union, readers are also invited to reflect on the conciliatory letter from the Westminster-based Pro United Kingdom Unionist Party (PUKUP). In an admirable gesture, PUKUP apologises for the involvement of Saxonia (previously known as England) in many of the 'unfortunate events' that have blighted Scottish history. PUKUP's letter is reproduced on page 5.

- An illustrated overview of how both sides envisage Scotland should they win the Referendum (see page 6). Paradoxically, their promises appear to be remarkably similar.

Yours faithfully

Rab Scallion
Chairman, Examination Board

THE BALLOT PAPER
Referendum on Scottish Independence
18th September 2014

Place your cross in the appropriate box

Nae cheatin or conferrin

Uryizup firrit?	
Aye	
Naw	
Mibbi aye mibbi naw	
Whoze askin	
Tellya ramorra	

PUKUP

The Pro UK Unionist Party

Dear Scotchmen

On behalf of Englishmen everywhere, we would like to offer an unreserved apology for our involvement in the following unfortunate events in Scottish history:

- Repeated and ultimately successful attempts to decimate Scotland's industrial base

- Always getting mixed up between the battles of Flodden and Culloden and between Edinburgh and Stirling castles

- Beating Scotland 9–3 at Wembley in 1961, although Scotland's 'goalkeeper' on the day must shoulder part of the blame

- Our drunken impersonations of Sean Connery

- Working in partnership with your clan chiefs to ethnically cleanse the Highlands

- The lack of taxis at Euston and King's Cross and their drivers' refusal to accept Royal Bank of Scotland notes

- Invading Edinburgh New Town every August while wearing raspberry-coloured cords

- The Bank of England for being just that

- The production of 'wreck-the-hoose juice' by the pious monks of Buckfast Abbey

- Beheading Mary, Queen of Scots, although ultimately it saved you the job

- The Windsor family's accent

- Lionising Baroness Thatcher as the saviour of the British economy when its real salvation was North Sea oil

- Piloting the Poll Tax on a very reluctant Scotland

- Sending Prince Charles to Gordonstoun

- Implying that the English never eat fried food and that the 'full English' is a vegetarian quiche

- The 1969 Monty Python sketch portraying Scots as the world's worst tennis players

Yours faithfully

M. Falange

Nigel Falange

What Both Sides are Promising for Post-Referendum Scotland

Curiously, both sides are promising voters exactly the same sort of post-Referendum Scotland. Below is an illustrated overview of their manifestos.

Before   **After**

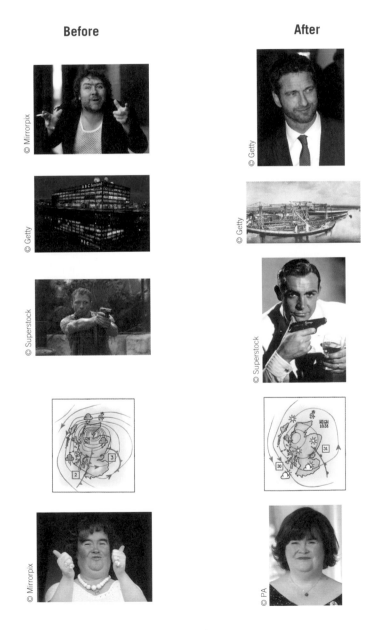

COMPLETING THE TEST

INSTRUCTIONS

- Candidates should at least attempt to read all of the questions

- Candidates have a fortnight to complete the test

- To avoid burnout, it is suggested that you only attempt one section at a time

- Please only use tartan ink

- Candidates may confer as they see fit, although this is unlikely to help

- Marks may be dedacted for bad spelling

- Due to budget cuts imposed by Saxonia, candidates are responsible for marking their own paper and the answers are given in Appendix 1

- All candidates with connections to Saxonia should automatically subtract twenty marks for consorting with the enemy

BONUS OPPORCHANCITIES

Candidates will also be asked to complete a set of more advanced questions. These Bonus Opporchancities are clearly marked throughout the paper. Subject to availability and the payment of a discretionary administration fee, candidates answering one or more of these questions successfully will be granted more than one vote.

STREET TALK

In several sections candidates are asked to answer a set of Street Talk questions. These are designed to measure applicants' awareness and understanding of day-to-day Scottish life. To comply with privacy laws, the names of actual commentators have been changed, for example:

'What about independence for the Kingdom of Fife?'
Nicky T. Nackity

'What a stramash this Referendum is causing.'
Kerr Fuffle

FREQUENTLY ASKED QUESTIONS

These are covered in Appendix 2 and include guidance on several key Referendum-related issues, for example:

Q: If we vote for Independence, will fry-ups still be kosher?

A: Technically speaking, fry-ups were never really kosher; however, current culinary practices will continue irrespective of the result, and south of Lanark couscous may be substituted for potato scones.

THE TEST'S MARKING SYSTEM

Including the bonus marks available in the Answers section, there are 300 marks available in the test. Page 105 sets this out in detail. Candidates scoring at least 150, or 50%, will be deemed to have passed. However, and irrespective of the scores achieved in other sections, a candidate will also be expected to score over 80% in the sections on Gender Studies and Scottish Sports Studies.

THE TEST PAPER

I. GENDER STUDIES

1.1 *The condition now known as Scottish Man Trance is reaching epidemic proportions. Which of the following two Scottish Man Trance incidents illustrated below caused serious collateral damage?*

(i) ☐

(ii) ☐

(2 marks)

1.2 From the exchange reported below, who was the most surprised?

(i) Tam ☐

(ii) Tam's wife ☐

(iii) The policeman ☐

Tam was walking home late at night when he saw a woman lurking in the shadows.

'Twenty quid,' she whispered.

Tam had never done this sort of thing before but thought, 'What the hell, it's only twenty quid,' so he joined her in the shadows.

They were only getting underway when they were caught in the glare of a powerful torch. It was a police officer.

'What's going on here?' asked the officer.

'I'm making love to my wife!' Tam answered, sounding annoyed.

'Oh, I'm so sorry,' said the policeman. 'I didn't realise.'

'Well, neither did I,' said Tam, 'until you shone that light in her face!'

(2 marks)

1.3 Up until the late 1970s, did the following quote accurately reflect the behaviour and beliefs of the average Scottish male?

(i) Yes ☐   (ii) No ☐

'God created woman because sheep can't type.'

(2 marks)

1.4 *Scotsmen have a reputation for engaging the ladies in conversation with their quick-witted banter. Which of the following two quotes illustrates this particularly endearing feature of the Scottish male?*

(i) 'I'll pretend to chat you up if you pretend to fancy me.' ☐

(ii) 'I'd try to chat you up, but I'm not sure you'd notice.' ☐

(2 marks)

Bonus Opporchancity

1.5 *A recent Strathsneckie University survey into the attitudes of Scottish women towards men provided several insights into the complexity of the female mind. Which one of the following two quotes is taken directly from that survey?*

(i) 'My husband said he needed more space, so I locked him outside.' ☐

(ii) 'Men who are lost never panic, they just change where they are going.' ☐

(2 marks)

1.6 *Recent medical research suggests that the quickest way to a Scotsman's heart is:*

(i) Through love ☐   (ii) Through his stomach ☐

(iii) Through his ribcage ☐

(2 marks)

1.7 Are all Scottish men quite so scheming?

(i) Absolutely ☐   (ii) Even worser ☐

A rather 'fit' young lady was about to undergo a minor operation in a Glasgow hospital and was wheeled down to the theatre. Before entering the room, the nurse left her outside while she went in to check that everything was ready for the operation.

Almost immediately, a serious-looking young man in a white coat approached the lady, pulled back the sheet and examined her closely. He looked puzzled and whispered to a colleague who was standing nearby. The second man came over and once again peeled back the sheet and had a close look at the lady.

Growing concerned, the lady asked, 'The examinations are appreciated, but at this late stage are they really necessary?'

The first man shrugged his shoulders and said, 'I've no idea, darling, we're just here to paint the ceiling.'

(2 marks)

1.8 Does the encounter described below suggest that marriage can be a cruel affair in Scotland?

(i) Yes ☐   (ii) Only if you're caught ☐

A woman was in bed with her lover. She was just telling him how stupid her husband was when the bedroom door flew open and there stood one very angry husband. He glared at his wife's lover and shouted, 'What are you doing here?'

'There,' said the wife to her lover. 'I told you he was stupid!'

(2 marks)

1.9 *MacSingles is Scotland's fastest-growing online and newspaper dating service. From the following selection of recently published 'male seeking female' adverts, candidates are asked to identify the ones they can best relate to. A glossary of frequently used terms and acronyms is provided for candidates who may be unfamiliar with the language used by MacSingles participants:*

MacSingles Dating: Some Frequently Used Terms

DDF	Disease- and drug-free	MBA	Married but available
DTM	Desperate to meet	MBP	Multiple body piercings
DW	Discernible waistline	RB	Rank badyin
FMHA	Full medical history available	SAE	Stamped addressed envelope
GCL	George Clooney lookalike	SSA	Social Services approved
		SUW	Scrubs up well

(i)　Reclusive social drinker from the Glasgow area and currently between jobs seeks lady in her early twenties who puts out on the first date and is interested in beer, Sky Sports, eating with her fingers. DDF. ☐

(ii)　MBA Maryhill intellectual seeks kindred spirit to complete Daily Record crossword. SSA certificate available for inspection. ☐

(iii)　Sexually overactive GCL Govan-based ski instructor and ex-test pilot with bedroom eyes seeks gullible young woman. FMHA if required. ☐

(iv)　Complex and often misunderstood Carluke man with diploma in Mood Management seeks completely different woman from the previous bitch. MBP but SUW. ☐

(v)　Delusional male, early sixties, DTM tactile blonde twins under thirty, preferably both female. ☐

(4 marks)

1.10 *Celibacy can either be a life choice or a condition imposed by circumstances. From the story below, which of the two applies to Hugh?*

(i) A life choice ☐   (ii) Imposed by circumstances ☐

While attending a marriage-guidance session, Hugh listened as the counsellor explained, 'In a marriage it is important that a couple understands the little things in life that are so important to each other.'

He then asked Hugh, 'Can you name your wife's favourite flower?'

Hugh smiled and while gently stroking his wife's hand answered, 'Self-raising?'

(2 marks)

1.11 *Was Bill's answer:*

(i) Harsh ☐   (ii) Harsh but correct ☐

Bill was sitting in the pub having a quiet drink with his wife when he unexpectedly announced, 'I love you.'

Somewhat taken aback, his wife asked, 'Is that the beer talking?'

Bill replied, 'No, it's me all right, but I'm talking to the beer.'

(2 marks)

1.12 Which of the following possibilities helps explain why Scotsmen often prefer their dog to their wife? Please tick two boxes as appropriate:

(i)   The later you are, the more excited the dog is to see you   ☐

(ii)   The dog does not notice when you call them by another dog's name   ☐

(iii) The dog's parents never visit   ☐

(iv) The dog does not wake you up and ask, 'If I died, would you ever get another dog?'   ☐

(2 marks)

TOTAL MARKS AVAILABLE FOR SECTION I: 26

THE CANDIDATE'S SCORE:

II. SCOTTISH LANGUAGE

2.1   *Although only forty miles apart, the citizens of Edinburgh and Glasgow often use different words to express the same meaning. Bearing this in mind, candidates are asked to consider whether the two lists below have been correctly labelled:*

(i) Yes ☐   (ii) No ☐

EDINBURGH	GLASGOW	EDINBURGH	GLASGOW
Special needs	Doolally	Freemasonry	The Craft
Academically challenged	Haddie	Queasy	The dry boak
Pale	Peely-wally	Plain	Hackit
Enthusiastic	Gie it laldy	Passed away	Deid
Pardon	Whit	Attractive	Stoatir

(2 marks)

2.2   *Irrespective of the result of the Referendum vote, will the two new words illustrated below be added to the next edition of the Scottish Dictionary?*

(i) Yes ☐   (ii) No ☐

Murrayhome (v)
To leave work early and rush home to watch Andy on TV

Andymonium (n)
Centre Court celebrations Sunday 7th July 2013, 5.23pm

(2 marks)

2.3   *Contradictions in terms, more properly known as oxymorons, are one of the many delights of the Scottish language. Which of the following two such expressions won the coveted Harsh But Fair award at the recent Edinburgh conference on the subject?*

(i) The Free Church ☐   (ii) The Clydeside Expressway ☐

(iii) Country music   ☐

(2 marks)

2.4 *Which other Scottish cities need the service illustrated below?*

(i) All of them ☐   (ii) All except Edinburgh ☐

Glasgow Council introduces a new service
for visitors to the Commonwealth Games

(2 marks)

2.5 *The following passage is taken from the evidence presented at a recent court case in Glasgow. The driver of a car had been pulled over by the police and the court was told that an animated conversation followed. Candidates are invited to agree or disagree with the Saxon translation of said conversation:*

(i) Agree ☐   (ii) Disagree ☐

SPEAKER	GLASWEGIAN	SAXON TRANSLATION
Policeman	Yallwrite?	Are you feeling all right?
Driver	Amawewrite.	I'm fine, thank you.
Policeman	Yeshoor?	Are you sure?
Driver	Aye.	Absolutely.
Policeman	Zisyoors?	Are you the owner of the vehicle?
Driver	Zwhitmine?	To what are you referring?
Policeman	Riscaur.	The vehicle.
Driver	Sibruririnlaw's.	Actually, it belongs to my sister's husband.
Policeman	Wershewren?	Where is he?
Driver	Raboozers.	In the pub.
Policeman	Yebingarglin?	Have you been drinking?
Driver	Jistacuppel.	Only two shandies.
Policeman	Yurstoatin.	You're drunk.
Driver	Nawamno.	I beg to differ.
Policeman	Yurstoatin.	I believe that I am spot on.
Driver	Umnoe.	I am sticking to my original story.

SPEAKER	GLASWEGIAN	SAXON TRANSLATION
Policeman	Geezusyerlizenz.	Can I see your driving licence?
Driver	Vnogoatwan.	I don't have one.
Policeman	Gerootramotir.	Get out of the car!
Driver	Whiffur?	Why?
Policeman	Mapolis.	I am a policeman.
Driver	Ommygoad.	Oh my god!
Policeman	Gerootwren.	Get out of the car.
Driver	Awritemcomin.	Certainly, officer, anything I can do to help.
Policeman	Blawrisup.	Will you please blow into the breathalyser?
Driver	Mgonnibesik.	I feel nauseous.
Policeman	Noovirmeyurno.	Not over me please.
Driver	Mawritenoo.	I'm feeling better now.
Policeman	Getinrapaddywagon.	Will you please get into the back of the van.
Driver	Werwigaun?	May I ask as to our destination?
Policeman	Rajile.	Headquarters.
Driver	Ommigoad ramissusill gimiadoin.	Oh my god, the lady of the house will not take kindly to this.
Policeman	Getinnawagon.	Could you get in the van please?
Driver	Niviragainratsitfurme.	I have learned a valuable lesson and alcohol will never again pass my lips.

(2 marks)

2.6 *Irrespective of September's Referendum result, will Scots and Saxons still be trading insults (see the illustration below) for centuries to come?*

(i) Yes ☐   (ii) No ☐

Despite global warming and rising sea levels
the rivalry continued till the bitter end

(2 marks)

2.7 *The Scottish language is always evolving. Please consider which of the following two recent additions to the country's 'wurds' you could see yourself using:*

(i) **Glibido:** The small talk used by Scotsmen when chatting up the ladies   ☐

(ii) **Negligent:** Scottish female habit of answering the door when wearing only a nightgown   ☐

(2 marks)

2.8 *When did adverts like this first appear in the Personals section of Scotland's major newspapers?*

(i) 1707 ☐   (ii) 2007 ☐

(2 marks)

2.9 Is it possible to translate this short exchange into standard Saxon?

(i) Yes ☐   (ii) No ☐

A Glasgow woman went into the butcher's shop. The owner had just come out of the freezer and was standing with his hands behind his back and his rear end strategically positioned in front of a small electric fire.

While looking at the display case, the woman innocently asked, 'Is that yer Ayrshire bacon?'

'Naw,' replied the butcher. 'It's jist ma hauns ah'm heatin'.'

(4 marks)

2.10 A young man was leaving a Glasgow city centre pub and was trying to retrieve his travel bag from under a table that was now occupied by a group of women. Please select which of the following two answers got the man into serious trouble with one of the women:

(i) Can I have my holdall?   ☐

(ii) Can I have my hole, doll?   ☐

(2 marks)

TOTAL MARKS AVAILABLE FOR SECTION II: 22

THE CANDIDATE'S SCORE:

III. POLITICS & INTERNATIONAL RELATIONS

3.1 *Could the cartoon below make all Scots vote 'yes' in September's Referendum?*

(i) Mibbi aye ☐

(ii) Mibbi naw ☐

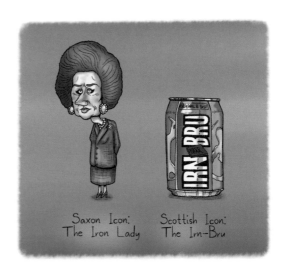

Saxon Icon: The Iron Lady   Scottish Icon: The Irn-Bru

(2 marks)

3.2 *In the run-up to the referendum, would Scots regard the Prime Minister's tactics as:*

(i) Praiseworthy ☐   (ii) Cynical ☐

David Cameron called Nick Clegg into his office and said, 'Nick, I think that we should make every effort to keep Scotland part of the UK.'

'I agree, but how can we do that?' replied Clegg.

'Well,' said Cameron, 'to look the part we'll get ourselves tweed jackets and a Scottie dog. Then, and having alerted the media, we'll go to a country pub in Glensomething-or-other to show that we really care about Scotland and that they should vote "no" in the Referendum.'

'Fantastic idea, Dave,' agreed Clegg.

So a few days later and all kitted out they set off with the media pack in tow and eventually they found a suitable country pub. They opened the door and casually strolled up to the bar.

'Good evening, landlord, two pints of beer please,' said Cameron.

'Good evening,' replied the landlord politely. 'Two pints coming up and perhaps some water for the wee dog.'

Cameron and Clegg stood leaning on the bar, taking care to nod every now and again to those coming in for a drink. Meanwhile, the dog lay quietly at their feet lapping up the water and the press pack took their photographs.

Suddenly the door from the adjacent lounge opened and in came an old shepherd. He walked up to the Scottie, lifted its tail with his crook and had a good look before shrugging his shoulders and walking back into the lounge. A few moments later, the local postman came in and followed the same procedure, much to the bewilderment of both Cameron and Clegg. This routine continued again and again with a number of customers repeating exactly the same thing. Eventually, and unable to stand it any longer, Clegg called over the landlord.

'Tell me', he said, 'why do people keep coming in and looking under the dog's tail like that? Is it some sort of Scottish custom?'

'Oh no,' said the landlord. 'It's just that somebody told them there was a dog in the bar with two arseholes . . .'

(2 marks)

3.3   If the SNP loses September's Referendum, could this be Alex Salmond's next job?

(i) Yes ☐   (ii) No ☐

(2 marks)

3.4   Traditionally, Scots are well known for their soldiering skills. Bearing this in mind, which of the following warzones have Scots recently served in?

(i) Sadr City, Iraq   ☐

(ii) Helmand Province, Afghanistan   ☐

(iii) A & E, Glasgow Royal Infirmary   ☐

(2 marks)

3.5 *Following the severe winter flooding in Saxonia (see map below), is the Independence Referendum still required?*

(i) Yes ☐   (ii) No ☐

(2 marks)

3.6 *Many observers believe that malapropisms[1] were invented specifically for some of Scotland's more confused politicians. Which of the following statements are largely thought to be genuine and which are merely playful urban myths?*

(i)   'I am resigning as union convenor and the chairman hopes
        to hold an erection soon.'   ☐

(ii)   'I can state, without any fear of contraception . . .'   ☐

(2 marks)

[1] Malapropism: the act of misusing words ridiculously, especially by confusing them
    with similar-sounding terms.

3.7 *Does the illustration below encapsulate Better Together's view about Scotland's sphere of influence in the world following any vote for Independence?*

(i) Yes ☐   (ii) No ☐

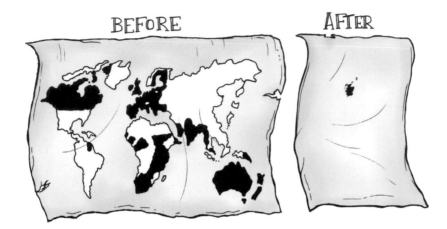

BEFORE   AFTER

(2 marks)

3.8 *In the question below, could you switch the names around depending on your political point of view?*

(i) Yes ☐   (ii) No ☐

Alex Salmond was visiting a primary school while one class was talking about words and their meanings. The teacher asked him if he would like to lead the discussion on the word 'tragedy'. The First Minister agreed and asked the class for an example of a tragedy.

A boy stood up and offered the following answer: 'If David Cameron was struck by lightning then that would be a tragedy.'

'Not so,' said Salmond. 'That would be an accident.'

A girl then raised her hand. 'If Nick Clegg and Ed Miliband were in a fatal car crash then that would be a tragedy.'

'I'm afraid not,' said Salmond, before explaining, 'That would be a great loss.'

Salmond searched the room for another volunteer, asking, 'Is there anyone in the class who can give me a really good example of a tragedy?'

Finally, from the back of the room a wee lad raised his hand and said, 'If a plane carrying you crashed then that would be a tragedy.'

'Quite right, young man!' exclaimed Salmond. 'Now, can you tell me why that would be a tragedy?'

'Well,' said the lad, 'it has to be a tragedy because it would certainly be no great loss and it probably wouldn't be an accident either!'

(2 marks)

3.9 What is wrong with this illustration?

(i) Alistair Darling is not really a badger ☐

(ii) The cull's on hold ☐

With the cull underway in Saxonia, refugees soon began arriving in Scotland

(4 marks)

Street Talk: The Referendum

3.10 Please tick the statements that you agree with:

(i) 'You can shove your Referendum where the sun don't shine.' ☐
Anne Enema

(ii) 'Leaving the UK would be a big mistake.' ☐
Polly C. Error

(iii) 'Maybe the Welsh will be next to ask whether they should remain a part of the UK.' ☐
Y.Y.Y. Delilah

(iv) 'If Scotland voted for Independence, would Saxonia invade?' ☐
Norman D. Landings

(2 marks)

3.11 Why did Edinburgh decide to build its ill-fated tram system (see below)?

(i) Glasgow did not have one ☐

(ii) Westminster was paying ☐

Edinburgh's pop-up book of tram mistakes

(2 marks)

3.12 Is this tale a pre-Referendum warning to all voters?

(i) Yes ☐   (ii) Yes, but it was ever thus ☐

A farmer was in a local pub when he struck up a conversation with a visitor, and before long the topic turned to politics.

The farmer said, 'Well, you know most politicians are Post Tortoises.'

Not being familiar with the term, the visitor asked him to explain what a Post Tortoise was.

The farmer replied, 'If you're walking down a country road and you come across a fence post with a tortoise balanced on the top of it then that's a Post Tortoise.'

The farmer, seeing the puzzled look on the visitor's face, explained, 'Well, you know the tortoise didn't get up there by himself. The tortoise doesn't belong up there and he doesn't know what to do while he's up there. He's elevated well beyond his station in life and you wonder what idiots put him there in the first place.'

(2 marks)

TOTAL MARKS AVAILABLE FOR SECTION III: 26

THE CANDIDATE'S SCORE:

IV. SCOTTISH MEDICINE & SCIENCE

4.1 *Male life expectancy in the East End of Glasgow is fifty-four, whereas in Chelsea and Kensington it is eighty-four. The thirty-year difference is largely explained by which of the following factors:*

(i) Bad luck ☐   (iii) Midges ☐

(ii) Ambushes ☐   (iv) A bad pint ☐

(2 marks)

4.2 *What percentage of the Tartan Army suffer from this debilitating form of psychological distress?*

(i) 10% ☐   (ii) 100% ☐

(2 marks)

Tartan Army on the Couch: No.1

I have this recurring nightmare that Archie Gemmill actually missed his wonder goal against Holland in 1978

4.3   *The World Health Organisation has identified a new football-related disease that only affects Scotsmen. The symptoms and circumstances of the ailment are detailed below. In medical circles, what has this disease been named?*

(i) Post Traumatic Stress Disorder   ☐

(ii) Déjà vu   ☐

(iii) Premature Jock Elation   ☐

- The Tartan Army walks around a foreign country sunburned, hungover and wearing ginger wigs.

- Although Scotland has only one point from its matches against the two 'weaker' teams, spirits are still high because if Scotland can beat the group's 'seeded' team 4–0 and other results go their way then they can still qualify.

- Scotland beat the 'seeded' team 4–0.

- The Tartan Army celebrates wildly, but due to a controversial equaliser in the clash of the two 'weaker' teams the other result does not go Scotland's way and the team crashes out of the competition.

- The Tartan Army listens with pride as the pundits praise how magnificent they have been and, after all, this was the Group of Death.

(4 marks)

4.4 *Which is the most popular form of birth control in Scotland?*

(i) The Buffalo Bill* ☐

(ii) The Susan Boyle* ☐

(iii) The Tartan Underwear ☐

*Hint for candidates: think Jockney rhyming slang

(2 marks)

4.5 *Which of the four strategies illustrated below offers the best known protection against midges?*

(i) ☐

(iii) ☐

(ii) ☐

(iv) ☐

(2 marks)

4.6 *What is the recognised medical term for an octogenarian in Glasgow's East End?*

(i) Lucky ☐   (ii) Unlucky ☐

(iii) Lost ☐   (iv) Tourist ☐

(2 marks)

4.7 *Scottish doctors are known for their brusque but practical bedside manner. Does the exchange below serve to reinforce this stereotype?*

(i) Yes ☐   (ii) No ☐

A consultant was doing his usual rounds in Glasgow's Southern General Hospital. He approached one of the patients, took one look at his charts and said, 'I have some bad and good news for you.'

The patient replies, 'So what's the bad news?'

The doctor says, 'We'll have to amputate both your legs.'

The patient replies, 'So what's the good news then?'

The doctor answers, 'The guy in the next bed wants to buy your slippers.'

(2 marks)

4.8 *In Scotland there is often more than one way of dealing with a medical emergency. Does the passage below illustrate this point?*

(i) Yes ☐   (ii) Yes, but actionable ☐

Morag was feeling very unwell and was rushed to hospital. After only three minutes in the examination room, the doctor explained to her that she was pregnant. Horrified by the news, Morag burst out of the room and ran down the corridor screaming.

The on-duty consultant stopped her, calmed her down and then asked what the problem was. After listening to her story, the consultant marched down the hallway and straight into the doctor's room.

'What's wrong with you?' he demanded. 'This woman is sixty-five years old, yet you told her that she was pregnant!'

Seemingly unconcerned by the consultant's ticking-off, the doctor replied, 'Does she still have her hiccups?'

(2 marks)

Street Talk: Scottish Health

4.9 *The following selection of emails to NHS 24 suggest that Scots suffer from many unusual medical conditions. Candidates are asked to tick all relevant boxes if they have suffered from the problems mentioned. Note that applicants ticking fewer than three boxes are unlikely to be viewed as having been completely honest:*

(i) 'How should Scots tackle their problems with alcohol?' ☐
Percy Veer, Bishopbriggs

(ii) 'The Scottish lifestyle is a recipe for disaster.' ☐
Al Deid, Barrhead

(iii) 'I have a recurring nightmare about swimming in the Clyde and being eaten by a giant fish.' ☐
Barry Cuda, Lanark

(iv) 'Since moving to Glasgow, I have had persistent problems with my tenses.' ☐
I Dunnit, Baillieston

(v) 'We always feel sick after eating pub lunches. What could be the cause?' ☐
Sam & Ella Sandwich, Govanhill

(2 marks)

4.10 *From the exchange below, was the librarian:*

(i) Harsh ☐   (ii) Technically correct ☐

A downcast and dishevelled man walked into a Glasgow library and asked the librarian, 'Excuse me, can ye lend us a book about toppin' yirsel'?'

The librarian slowly looked him up and down disdainfully before replying, 'Naw, cos ye'll no bring it back!'

(2 marks)

4.11 *Do you think that back at home the Saxonian's member would have been considered:*

(i) Small ☐   (ii) Average ☐   (iii) Large ☐

'Of course I won't laugh,' said the Glaswegian nurse. 'I'm a professional and in over twenty years at the Southern General I've never laughed at a patient, let alone a tourist from south of the border.'

'Okay then,' said Fred, and he proceeded to drop his trousers, revealing a miserable member no bigger than an AAA battery.

Unable to control herself, the nurse started giggling but quickly regained her composure and apologised. 'I'm sorry, I don't know what came over me, but I promise that won't happen again. Now, what seems to be the problem?'

'It's swollen,' Fred replied.

(2 marks)

TOTAL MARKS AVAILABLE FOR SECTION IV: 24

THE CANDIDATE'S SCORE:

V. SOCIOLOGY

5.1 Does Murray have a precocious sense of humour?

(i) Absolutely ☐

The only way for the McGregors to pull off a Sunday afternoon 'quickie' with their young son Murray in the flat was to send him out on to the balcony, give him a Mars Bar and ask him to eat it slowly and report on the goings-on in the street below.

Without further ado, Murray began his commentary and his parents put their plan into operation.

'Mr Jones is washing his car.'

'Looks like the Andersons have visitors.'

'Oli's riding his bike.'

'The Sanders are going out.'

'Andy's on his skateboard!'

'Sammy's playing football with his brother.'

'Mary's taking her dog for a walk.'

Then, after a brief pause, he announced, 'The Coopers are shagging!'

Startled by this, the parents stopped their romancing and the father called out, 'Murray, how do you know what they're doing?'

'Jimmy Cooper's standing on his balcony eating a Mars Bar!'

(2 marks)

5.2   Please study the illustration below and decide whether Relate is:

(i) A distant relative ☐   (ii) Too little too late ☐

"Maybe we should consider seeing Relate?"

(2 marks)

5.3 *Candidates are asked to match the following two short stories with two of Scotland's most admired character traits:*

(i) Quick thinking ☐   (ii) Pragmatism ☐

A   A Scotsman was driving south to London through Yorkshire while a local was driving in the opposite direction. They hit each other head-on and both cars were a total write-off. Eventually, the Scotsman managed to climb out of his car and survey the damage. Badly shaken, he looked at the twisted wreckage of his car and thought, 'I'm really lucky to be alive!'

A few minutes later, the Saxon scrambled out from his car, looked at the wreckage and said, 'I just can't believe I survived this accident without a scratch!'

The Saxon walked over to the Scotsman and said, 'You know, I think this is a sign that we should put aside our petty differences and live as friends instead of rivals.'

The Scotsman reflected for a moment and replied, 'You're absolutely right! We should be friends. Let's check if anything can be saved from the wreckage.'

After a struggle, the Scotsman managed to open the boot of his car and miraculously found a bottle of whisky still intact. Waving the bottle, he called over to his newfound Saxon friend. 'I think this is yet another sign that we should be friends and I say that we toast our newfound understanding.'

The Saxon said, 'You're right!' and he accepted the bottle from the Scotsman and started to drink the whisky. After knocking back nearly half the bottle, the Saxon then handed it back to the Scotsman and said, 'Your turn!'

The Scotsman twisted the cap back on the bottle and said, 'Nah, I'm okay, thanks; I think we should just sit down and wait for the police to show up.'

B A notorious robber went into the Royal Bank of Scotland's Paisley branch and produced a gun and demanded all their money. Unfortunately, as he was making his getaway, his mask slipped, revealing his face. Panicking, he turned to a customer in the queue and barked, 'Did you see my face?'

The man replied, 'Yes, I'm afraid I did.'

Immediately, the bank robber shot him. He then turned to a couple who had also been queuing and asked the man the same question: 'Did you see my face?'

Nervously, but without hesitating, the man replied, 'No, but the wife did.'

(2 marks)

5.4 *Please read the short passage below and decide what is the moral of the story:*

(i) Beware predatory males ☐

(ii) One good turn deserves another ☐

A young Glasgow girl who was down on her luck decided to end it all one night by throwing herself into the Clyde. As she stood on the edge of the river, a young sailor noticed her and asked, 'You're not thinking of jumping, are you?'

'Yes, I am,' replied the sobbing girl.

Putting his arm around her, the sailor coaxed her back from the brink and said, 'Look, nothing's worth that. I'll tell you what: we're sailing off for America tomorrow. Why don't I help you stow away and you can start a new life in the States. I'll set you up in one of the lifeboats, bring you food and water every night, and I'll look after you if you look after me – if you know what I mean.'

The girl agreed and the sailor sneaked her on board that very night. For the next week the sailor came to her lifeboat every night, bringing food and water and then making love to her. Then, during the second week, the captain got wind of the goings-on and checked the lifeboat. He pulled back the lifeboat's cover and found the girl. He demanded an explanation and the startled girl confessed all: 'I wanted to begin a new life in America so one of the sailors smuggled me on board and, in return for bringing me food every night, he's been screwing me.'

The captain paused for a moment before replying, 'He certainly has been, sweetheart. This is the Dunoon ferry.'

(2 marks)

5.5 *In the exchange below, is Fraser being:*

(i) Sarcastic ☐   (ii) Frugal ☐

One of Fraser's friends called by to find him and his family stripping the wallpaper from every room in the house.

'You're decorating, then?' asked the friend.

'No, we're flitting,' replied Fraser.

(2 marks)

5.6 *Based on the illustration below, was Strathclyde's decision to opt for the industrial-strength taser too extreme?*

(i) Yes ☐   (ii) No ☐

(2 marks)

5.7 Do you think that Big Tam was being:

(i) Racist ☐   (ii) Merely pragmatic ☐

Big Tam was standing in a bar in Glasgow minding his own business when a Chinese guy wandered in, stood next to him and started drinking a beer.

Tam nonchalantly asked him, 'Do you know any of thae martial arts things, like kung fu, karate or ju-jitsu?'

Annoyed at being racially stereotyped, the Chinese guy replied, 'No, and why did you ask me that? Is it just because I look Chinese?'

'No,' said Tam casually, 'It's because yiv jist drunk ma beer!'

(2 marks)

5.8 Is the short exchange below a typical Scottish male response to a common family problem?

(i) Yes ☐   (ii) No ☐

A wife announced to her husband that she was expecting their fourth child and suggested that they move house.

The husband replied, 'There's no point, they'll find us eventually.'

(2 marks)

5.9 *Scotsmen are renowned for their strength and masculinity. Does the following story further enhance their reputation?*

(i) Yes ☐   (ii) No ☐

A trucker drove into a small town in the American Midwest where a circus was in full swing. A sign read: 'Don't Miss the Amazing Scot'. Intrigued, the trucker bought a ticket and took his seat in the arena.

In the centre of the circus ring there was a table with three walnuts on it. Standing next to the table was an old kilted Scot. Suddenly the old man lifted his kilt, whipped out a massive member and smashed all the walnuts to pieces with three mighty swings! The audience erupted into applause and the Scot was carried off shoulder-high by the crowd.

Ten years later, the trucker visited the same town and saw the same sign for the same circus: 'Don't Miss the Amazing Scot'. He could not believe the old fellow was still alive, let alone still doing his act, so he bought a ticket and went in to see the show. Once again, the table was in the centre of the circus ring, but this time instead of walnuts there were three coconuts on the table. The Scot stood in front of them with his eyes closed, deep in concentration. Suddenly he lifted his kilt and shattered the coconuts with three swings of his massive member. The crowd went wild and once again the Scot was carried shoulder-high from the arena!

Flabbergasted, the trucker tracked him down after the show. 'You're incredible!' he told the Scot. 'But I have to know something. You're much older than the last time I saw you, yet you've switched from walnuts to coconuts?'

'Well, son,' said the Scot with a hint of sadness in his voice, 'ma eyes urnie whit they used tae be.'

(2 marks)

5.10 Whose magic trick was the best?

(i) The Saxon ☐   (ii) The Scotsman ☐

A Scotsman and a Saxon went down to the pub. As soon as he got to the bar, the Saxon whisked three pies off the counter and into his pocket without the barman even noticing.

He then said to the Scotsman, 'You see how clever we Saxons are? You'll never beat that!'

Never one to shirk from a challenge, the Scotsman said, 'Watch this.'

He said to the barman, 'If you give me a pie, I'll show you some magic!'

Happy to go along with the fun, the barman gave him a pie. The Scotsman wolfed it down and immediately said to the barman, 'If you give me another pie, I'll show you some more magic.'

Although the barman was confused, he still gave the Scotsman a second pie. The Scotsman ate it and then immediately asked for a third pie. Despite his mounting suspicions, the barman obliged and the Scotsman duly devoured it.

By now the barman was feeling duped and asked, 'So what about the magic, then?'

The Scotsman smiled and said, 'Just have a look in the Saxon's pocket!'

(4 marks)

TOTAL MARKS AVAILABLE FOR SECTION V: 22

THE CANDIDATE'S SCORE:

VI. MODERN STUDIES

6.1 *Which of the following Scottish foods have recently been accorded the EU's much sought-after Protected Designation of Origin status, as has been conferred upon champagne and Parma ham?*

(i) Tunnock's Caramel Wafers ☐   (iii) Stovies ☐

(ii) Well-fired morning rolls ☐   (iv) Lamb rogan josh ☐

(2 marks)

6.2 *At the Annual MacCrufts Show at Glasgow's SECC, which of the following dogs did not reach the final round of Top Status Dog in Show?*

(i) Felony, Ferguslie Park ☐

(iii) Alibi, Craigmillar ☐

(ii) Fifi, Morningside ☐

(iv) Nitro, Easterhouse ☐

(4 marks)

42

6.3 *To comply with health and safety concerns, the number 20 bus to Drumchapel has recently been equipped with a rear gunner:*

(i) True ☐   (ii) False ☐

(2 marks)

6.4 *Which of the following are traditional and much-loved Paisley proverbs?*

(i) Those who live by the sword get shot by those who don't ☐

(ii) Familiarity breeds . . . ☐

(iii) An ASBO in time saves nine ☐

(iv) Check the DNA before rather than after the christening ☐

(2 marks)

6.5 *Which of these images do Scots often hang over the mantelpiece to keep their kids away from the fire?*

© Getty Editorial

(i) ☐

© Getty

(iii) ☐

(ii) ☐

© Getty

(iv) ☐

(2 marks)

6.6 Scotland's definition of a heatwave is:

(i) A foreign holiday ☐   (ii) The menopause ☐

(iii) A two-bar electric fire ☐

(2 marks)

6.7 How many did the police successfully breathalyse in Larkhall?

(i) Zero ☐   (ii) Less than one ☐

An unmarked police car was parked outside a popular Larkhall pub. At about 11 p.m. one of the officers noticed Stu leaving the bar so drunk that he could barely walk. Stu stumbled around the car park for a few minutes while awkwardly trying his keys on several vehicles before he finally found his car. He eventually managed to open the door and then slumped into the driver's seat. He composed himself for a few minutes while also waving to several other patrons as they left the bar to drive home.

Finally Stu started his car but not before mistakenly switching the windscreen wipers and hazard lights on and off repeatedly. Ever so slowly he inched the car forward, then stopped to allow a few more cars out of the pub's car park. Finally, Stu summoned the courage to pull out of the car park and he drove off erratically down the road.

The police followed Stu for a while before pulling him over and breathalysing him. To their amazement, the result was negative and one officer said, 'Sorry, we'll have to ask you to accompany us to the police station for a blood test – our equipment must be broken.'

'I doubt it,' said Stu. 'I'm tonight's designated decoy.'

(4 marks)

Street Talk: Scotland's Youth

6.8 *Which of the following comments characterise the youth of today?*

(i) 'The neds are taking over.' ☐
Dylan Quints, Partick

(ii) 'Young hooligans are everywhere.' ☐
Ned Ridden, Bishopston

(2 marks)

6.9 *Does the phrase 'not up, not in' refer to:*

(i) A well-known putting tip ☐

(ii) The motto of the Eastercraigs erectile-dysfunction clinic ☐

(2 marks)

6.10 *Did this story win Scotland's Chauvinists' Joke of the Year in 2013?*

(i) Yes ☐   (ii) No ☐

A blonde woman was speeding down the road and was pulled over by a blonde woman police officer. The blonde cop asked to see the blonde driver's licence, but, although she rummaged through her handbag, she could not find it.

Growing increasingly agitated, the driver finally asked the policewoman for help: 'Can you remind me what it looks like?'

The policewoman replied through gritted teeth, 'It's square and it has your picture on it.'

The driver finally found a small mirror in her handbag and took one look at it before handing it to the policewoman. 'Here it is,' she said with a sense of satisfaction.

The blonde officer looked at the mirror, then handed it back, saying, 'Okay, you can go, I didn't realise you were one of us.'

(2 marks)

6.11 Which of the following was the Edinburgh Fringe's funniest one-liner in 2011?

(i) They asked for a password eight characters long, so I chose Snow White and the Seven Dwarfs. ☐

(ii) Theft from multi-storey car parks is wrong on several levels. ☐

(iii) People often say that they're taking it one day at a time, but that's just how time works. ☐

(2 marks)

TOTAL MARKS AVAILABLE FOR SECTION VI: 26

THE CANDIDATE'S SCORE:

7.1 *Which of the following two churches has the higher membership in Scotland?*

(i) The Church of Scotland ☐

(ii) The Church of Maradona ☐

(2 marks)

Bonus

7.2 *Explain why when a Scot moves to Saxonia the average IQ of both countries increases. Answer in the space provided and please show all your workings.*

(4 marks)

7.3 *From the passage below, candidates are invited to decide whether in Scotland material concerns sometimes override religious beliefs.*

(i) Absolutely ☐

The daughter of a strict Catholic family had not been home for years. On her return, her father immediately took her to task.

'Where have you been all this time? Why did you not write to us? Why didn't you call or text? Do you not understand what you've put your mother through?'

Through her tears the girl replied, 'Dad . . . I became a prostitute and I was too ashamed to come home or even contact you.'

'You what?! Get out of this house! You're a disgrace to this family!' the father shouted.

'All right, as you wish. I only came back to give you the title deeds to a house I bought you. And for my little brother, this Rolex, and for you, Dad, the new Mercedes that's parked outside,' she replied.

Pausing for a moment, the father then asked, 'Now, what was it you said that you'd become?'

Sobbing, the girl said, 'A prostitute, Dad, a prostitute!'

'Oh, you scared me half to death, girl! I thought you said a Protestant! Come here and give your dad a hug.'

(2 marks)

Bonus

7.4 *In Scotland, distance is measured in minutes, so what is time measured in? Answer in the space provided and please show all your workings.*

(4 marks)

7.5 *If Old McDonald laid every sheep on his farm end to end, would he be arrested?*

(i) Absolutely ☐   (ii) Absolutely not ☐

(2 marks)

7.6 *'The hawk never hears the sparrow's prayers' is the motto of which Scottish organisation?*

(i) The Samaritans ☐

(ii) The Faculty of Advocates ☐

(iii) The Scottish Payday Loan Association ☐

(2 marks)

7.7 *Candidates are asked to examine the photograph below and answer:*

a) How many midges can you see?

(i) 0 ☐   (ii) 1 ☐

b) How many midges are actually there?

(i) 10,000 ☐   (ii) 20,000 ☐

(iii) 30,000 ☐   (iv) 300,000 ☐

© Getty

(4 marks)

7.8 *The teacher asked Billy, 'If you have five sweets and Tom asks for one, how many sweets will you have left?' What was Billy's answer?*

(i) Five ☐

(ii) Other than five ☐

(2 marks)

TOTAL MARKS AVAILABLE FOR SECTION VII: 22

THE CANDIDATE'S SCORE:

VIII. SCOTTISH HISTORY, CULTURE & THE ARTS

8.1 **Which Scottish general killed the most Saxon soldiers?**

(i) William Wallace (1272–1305) ☐

(ii) Robert the Bruce (1312–1314) ☐

(iii) Earl Haig (1914–1918) ☐

(2 marks)

8.2 **Which of the two following figures from history are unlikely Scottish heroes?**

(i) William the Conqueror ☐

(ii) Joan of Arc ☐

(2 marks)

8.3 **Scotland's primary role in the building of the British Empire was to provide:**

(i) Civil servants ☐   (ii) Bankers ☐

(iii) Accountants ☐   (iv) Cannon fodder ☐

(2 marks)

8.4 *Which of the following are the two greatest movies ever made?*

(i) *Citizen Kane* ☐   (iii) *The Third Man* ☐

(ii) *Vertigo* ☐   (iv) *Gregory's Girl* ☐

(4 marks)

8.5 *Which of the following were world-famous Scottish male ballet dancers?*

(i)   (iii)

(ii)   (iv)

(2 marks)

8.6 *Wishaw is a town now best known as a popular stop-off on Scotland's Industrial Heritage Trail. Which of the following two sayings relates to the town's illustrious past?*

(i) All roads lead to Wishaw ☐

(ii) Wishaw was not built in a day ☐

(2 marks)

8.7 Which of the following Tartan Army choruses from the 1970s are now popular Scottish ringtones?

(i) We're on the march with Ally's Army,
We're on the way to the Argentine ☐

(ii) Tom Forsyth, he's called jaws,
He's got Channon by the baws ☐

(iii) Bobby Moore, superstar,
Walks like a woman and he wears a bra ☐

(2 marks)

8.8 Is the following a true story?

(i) Absolutely ☐

After centuries of fighting, the McDonalds and the Campbells finally signed a truce. To cement the agreement, a marriage was soon arranged between the son and daughter of the two clan chiefs.

Young Callum McDonald, the bridegroom-to-be, understood the politics behind the marriage, but he was concerned that his Campbell bride might not be a virgin. With this preying on his mind, he sought the advice of an old shepherd who was the wisest member of the clan. The shepherd immediately grasped the problem and advised, 'Listen, Callum, the clan has a fail-safe virginity test that only requires one pot of red dye, one pot of blue dye and a shovel.'

Young Callum looked bemused and asked the shepherd, 'And exactly what am I to do with these?'

The shepherd replied, 'Before you climb into bed on your wedding night, you paint one of your balls red and the other blue. If the Campbell woman says, "That's the strangest pair of balls, I ever saw," you hit her very hard on the head with the shovel and run for it.'

(2 marks)

8.9 *Is* **Fifty Shades of Tartan** *a sadomasochistic book about:*

(i) Tartan ☐

(ii) Scottish relationships ☐

(iii) The national football team ☐

(4 marks

TOTAL MARKS AVAILABLE FOR SECTION VIII: 22

THE CANDIDATE'S SCORE:

IX. BUSINESS & BANKING

9.1 *The collapse of HBOS in 2008 was caused by:*

(i) Fred Goodwin ☐   (ii) Margaret Thatcher ☐

(2 marks)

Street Talk: Scottish Banking

9.2 *Which of the following Street Talk comments could apply to banking and bankers?*

(i) 'Despite losing billions, no banker has yet been charged with an offence.'
Y. Knott, Methil ☐

(ii) 'To conceal their ill-gotten gains, I suspect that many bankers will have set up offshore bank accounts.'
Isla Man, Douglas ☐

(iii) 'Bankers have only succeeded in taking from the poor and giving to the rich.'
Robin Hoods, Banchory ☐

(2 marks)

9.3 *Does the story reproduced below suggest that the years spent training Dunkie were wasted?*

(i) Yes ☐   (ii) No ☐

Dunkie and his mate were working for Livingston New Town's Roads Department. Dunkie would dig a hole by the side of the street and his mate would follow behind and fill the hole in. They worked all the way up one side of the street and then down the other before moving on. They both laboured away all day with Dunkie digging a hole and his mate then filling it in.

A passer-by who couldn't understand the point of the exercise finally asked Dunkie, 'I don't get it. Why do you dig a hole only to have the other guy fill it up again?'

Dunkie explained, 'Well, we're normally a three-man team, but the bloke who plants the trees called in sick today.'

(2 marks)

Street Talk: Fred Goodwin

9.4 *Which of the following Street Talk comments about Fred Goodwin do you agree with?*

(i)   'Most people were delighted when Goodwin left the
Royal Bank.'   ☐
Gladys Allover, Merchiston

(ii) 'The media has got it in for Fred.'   ☐
Roger D. Goodwin, Gogarburn

(iii) 'Goodwin's time at the Royal Bank was a disaster.'   ☐
Beyoncé Pale, Brechin

(2 marks)

9.5 When will Scotland's oil reserves run out?

(i) Sometime between 2140 and 2145 ☐

(ii) As soon as Scotland votes for Independence ☐

(4 marks)

9.6 What is the difference between a supermarket trolley and a non-executive director of a Scottish bank?

(i) Everything ☐

(ii) You regularly fill them both with food and drink, but a supermarket trolley often has a mind of its own ☐

(2 marks)

9.7 *What percentage of overseas visitors to Scotland have faced the same problem as ET?*

(i) 0% ☐   (ii) 100% ☐

Tourist faces bankruptcy over roaming charges

(2 marks)

9.8 In the story below, how do you think the 'wee Weegie woman' reached her conclusion?

(i) Instinctively ☐   (ii) Phoned a friend ☐

Two Edinburgh men were sitting down for a coffee break while setting up their new shop in Glasgow's Argyle Street.

One said to the other, 'I bet any minute now a nosey wee Weegie woman is going to walk by and ask what we're going to be selling.'

No sooner were the words out of his mouth when, sure enough, a nosey wee Weegie woman walked in the door and asked, 'What are you two gonna be selling here then?'

One of the men replied sarcastically, 'Arseholes.'

In the blink of an eye the wee Weegie woman replied, 'You're doing well, lads, only two left!'

(2 marks)

Street Talk: The Economic Downturn

9.9 Which of the following comments ring true?

(i) 'When times are tough, the government should do
more to protect Scotland's rich fishing grounds.'
Fraser Brough, Arbroath ☐

(ii) 'During the recession, Scots should just buy cheaper
clothes.'
Polly Ester, Leith ☐

(iii) 'If this recession continues, then parts of Scotland
could face civil unrest.'
Mandy Barricades, Tarbert ☐

(2 marks)

9.10 Based on the illustration below, are Scottish banks in danger of taking their money-laundering checks too far?

(i) Can't be too careful these days ☐

(ii) It's even more worser ☐

The Bank's money laundering team grills the toothfairy about her source of funds.

(2 marks)

TOTAL MARKS AVAILABLE FOR SECTION IX: 24

THE CANDIDATE'S SCORE:

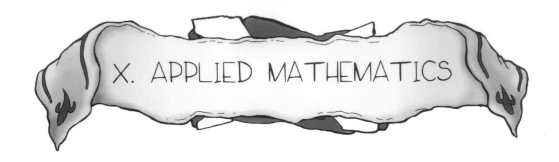

X. APPLIED MATHEMATICS

10.1 Deeks and Dobbie were convicted of dealing drugs. Deeks was sentenced to eighteen months in jail but Dobbie got three years. Did Dobbie receive a harsher sentence because:

(i) He had several previous convictions ☐

(ii) The judge had other information ☐

(4 marks)

10.2 *When Rangers play Celtic, Rangers fans sing the Sash every ten minutes when they're winning and every fifteen minutes when they're losing. Bearing that in mind, how many times will they sing their party piece during a 0–0 draw?*

(i) 9 ☐   (iii) Constantly ☐

(ii) 6 ☐   (iv) Never ☐

(2 marks)

10.3 *Dixie faced a dilemma. He reckoned he would receive £13.50 a week in Married Couple's Allowance if he tied the knot with Anne Marie. However, he calculated that even if he managed to borrow the ring and got the required recreational drugs at a discount, the wedding would still cost him £250. Of more concern, he would have to start buying two fish suppers at £3.50 each every night instead of the one he was currently living on. From a financial perspective, how long would it be before Dixie wished that he had stayed single?*

(i) Immediately ☐   (ii) As soon as he sobers up ☐

(2 marks)

10.4 *In certain deprived areas of the Central Belt, Senga Sudoku is one of the favourite pastimes of females, but all Scots are expected to be at ease with the mathematical concepts involved. Bearing this in mind, please complete the following 'expert' Senga Sudoku puzzle:*

1	3	6	7	8	2	9	5	4
5	2	9	4	1	3	6	8	7
7	8	4	9	6	5	2	1	3
7	8	4	9	6	5	2	1	3
6	5	8	1		7	4	3	2
4	7	3	2	5	8	1	9	6
8	4	5	3	2	9	7	6	1
2	9	1	5	7	6	3	4	8
3	6	7	8	4	1	5	2	9

(4 marks)

10.5 *Magnus from Morningside worked out that 50% of his friends said that they went to school with Ewan McGregor. A further 33% claimed that their uncle went to university with Gordon Brown. Moreover, exactly 25% said that their dad played rugby against Tony Blair and 40% said that Sean Connery was their milkman. Based on the above, what percentage of Magnus's friends claim to know Susan Boyle?*

(i) 100% ☐   (ii) 0% ☐

(2 marks)

10.6 Were the bookies' calculations correct?

(i) Yes ☐   (ii) No ☐

After months of research the bookies have installed
Celtic as favourites to win the Scottish Premier League

(2 marks)

10.7 A summary of a local authority tendering process is presented below and candidates are asked to decide who won the contract:

(i) Tam ☐   (ii) Bennie ☐   (iii) Banjo ☐

Tam, Bennie and Banjo were called into the local council's offices to tender for some minor housing repairs. Tam was first in and was asked what his tender was by the committee's chairman. '£30,000, councillor,' he responded. He was then asked by the councillor if he could be more specific, so he replied, '£10,000 for materials, £10,000 for labour and £10,000 for maself.'

Bennie was next in and was asked what his quote was. He responded, '£60,000, councillor,' and once again he was asked if he could be more specific, so Bennie replied '£20,000 for materials, £20,000 for labour and £20,000 for maself.'

Finally it was Banjo's turn and he was asked what his quote was. Banjo replied, '£90,000, councillor.' The councillor was clearly a bit taken aback by the cost of his scheme, so he asked Banjo if he could be more specific. Banjo replied, '£30,000 for you, £30,000 for me, and we'll get Tam tae do the work.'

(2 marks)

10.8 This is a three-part question. After a long Friday night in his local, Spike began his walk home. Spike lived 200 yards down the road from the pub, but his direction of travel was impaired by alcohol. Indeed, for every two steps that Spike took forward he took one step to the side and then one step back. If Spike's stride is eighteen inches long then please answer the following:

(a) How many steps did it take for Spike to get home?

(i) 1,594   ☐   (ii) 1,595   ☐

(iii) 1,596   ☐   (iv) 1,597   ☐

(b) If Spike discovered that he'd left his house keys in the pub, how many additional steps did he need to take to solve his problem?

(i) 1,594 x 2   ☐   (ii) 1,595 x 2   ☐

(iii) 1,596 x 2   ☐   (iv) 1,597 x 2   ☐

(c) If each of Spike's steps took a minute to execute, approximately how long did it take him to get home?

(i) The entire weekend   ☐

(4 marks)

TOTAL MARKS AVAILABLE FOR SECTION X: 22

THE CANDIDATE'S SCORE:

11.1 Which one of the world's top ten football teams is prone to be 2–0 up at half-time and yet lose the match to a hotly contested injury-time goal?

(i) Brazil ☐   (ii) Spain ☐

(iii) Netherlands ☐   (iv) Scotland ☐

(2 marks)

11.2 Please study the illustration below and decide whether this really happened in this pre-1990 job interview for Rangers FC:

(i) No ☐   (ii) Yes ☐

"Superman, you seem well qualified tae play for the Rangers but could you remind us again whit school you went tae."

(2 marks)

11.3 Which two of the following football-related quotes were NOT made by a Scot:

(i) 'They'll be dancing on the streets of Raith tonight.' ☐

(ii) 'To be second with one game to go – you can't ask for anything more than that.' ☐

(iii) 'I felt that the only real difference between Scotland and Saxonia were the goals that Saxonia scored.' ☐

(iv) 'Yes, it looks as if Hearts have reverted to a five-man back four.' ☐

(2 marks)

11.4 Does the following story suggest that a Scotsman's instinct for self-preservation can occasionally even trump tribal loyalties?

(i) Yes ☐   (ii) No ☐

Ali and Pat, two Celtic supporters, were heading to Hampden for a cup final against Rangers, but when they went through the turnstile they discovered they were in the wrong end of the ground! So Ali suggested to Pat, 'We'd better keep our scarves in our pockets and we can slowly make our way over to the Celtic end, and safety.' However, before they were able to execute their plan, Celtic scored.

Several hours later, Pat woke up in hospital, covered head to toe in plaster and with a concerned Ali by his bedside.

'Are ye awright?' Ali asked.

'Aye, but whit happened?' Pat replied.

Ali said, 'Well, when we tried to make oor way over to oor end, Celtic scored and you jumped up in the air to celebrate.'

'Now I remember, but how come you're all right?' asked the injured Pat.

His mate replied sheepishly, 'Well, ah wis the first wan tae steam intae ye!'

(2 marks)

11.5 Will Jake ever master scuba diving?

(i) No ☐   (ii) Don't underestimate Jake ☐

Jake decided to go on a scuba-diving course. On the first day the instructor asked his class why divers should always fall backwards off the boat into the sea.

Jake immediately answered, 'Well, if they fell forward they'd still be in the boat.'

(2 marks)

11.6 Which of the following was the Tartan Army's official response to the referee's decision disallowing Frank Lampard's 'over-the-line' goal against Germany in the 2010 World Cup finals?

(i) Guttedsoweeswaz   ☐

(ii) Ah couldnae see it maself, need tae havaluke onra video ☐

(iii) Refreezs deshizins finill, byrawhey   ☐

(2 marks)

11.7 *In spicing up the high diving event (see below), do you think that the organisers of the Glasgow Commonwealth Games will succeed in attracting a larger share of the national TV audience?*

(i) Yes ☐   (ii) No ☐

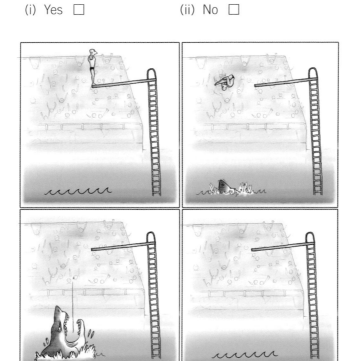

High Diving the Glasgow Games 2014

(2 marks)

11.8 Which two of the following goalkeepers have recently been inducted into the Scottish Football Hall of Fame?

(i) Frank Haffey (1961)
Scotland 3, Saxonia 9 □

(iii) Stewart Kennedy (1975)
Scotland 1, Saxonia 5 □

(ii) Scott Carson (2007)
Saxonia vs Croatia □

(iv) Robert Green (2010)
Saxonia vs USA □

(2 marks)

11.9 Was the dog's first or second footballing answer correct?

(i) The first, while in the bar □

(ii) The second, while out on the street □

Donnie walked into a pub with his dog under his arm. He sat down at the bar and put the dog on the stool next to him. The barman said, 'Sorry, no dogs allowed.'

Donnie replied, 'But this is a special dog – he can talk!'

'Pull the other one,' said the barman. 'Now out of here the both of you before I have to throw you out.'

'No, wait,' said Donnie, 'I'll prove it.'

He turned to his dog and asked, 'What do you find on top of a house?'

'Woof!' said the dog, wagging his tail.

'Listen, pal . . .' said the barman, clearly losing his patience.

'No, wait,' said Donnie, 'I'll ask him another question'.

And he turned to the dog and said, 'What noise does a fire make?'

'Woof!' barked the dog, wagging his tail.

'Look, stop wasting my time and get out of here!' said the barman.

'One more chance,' pleaded Donnie and, turning to the dog, he asked, 'Who is the greatest-ever Scottish goalkeeper?'

The dog looked at him closely and barked, 'Ruff!' while wagging his tail.

'Okay, that's it!' said the barman, and he threw Donnie and his dog out of the pub.

After licking his wounds, the dog turned to his owner and said, 'Do you think I should have answered Andy Goram?'

(2 marks)

11.10 *Given the country's many alpine resorts, Scots are particularly adept at winter sports. From the photographs below, which one is the Scot and which is the Saxon?*

(i) Alain Baxter ☐   (ii) Eddie the Eagle   ☐

(2 marks)

11.11 *As the photograph immediately below illustrates, shinty is often said to personify a Scotsman's rugged and combative personality. Which of the two other pictures illustrate the equivalent 'contact' sport in Saxonia?*

(i) ☐   (ii) ☐

(2 marks)

11.12 *Was the Memory Man correct about the Partick Thistle goal?*

(i) Yes ☐ (ii) No ☐

Murdo was in the south-western USA on his annual sales trip from Scotland to the region. At the weekend, Murdo drove out to a remote town, checked into the only hotel and then headed for the only bar.

Once inside, he ordered a drink and then noticed a Native American chief, dressed in his full regalia and standing under a sign saying, 'Ask me anything, paleface.'

Murdo was intrigued and asked the barman about him.

'He's Red Cloud, the Memory Man. Red Cloud knows everything and he's never been stumped for an answer to any question,' said the barman.

'He knows everything?' asked Murdo.

'Yes, he knows every fact there is to know and he never forgets anything,' said the barman.

'No way,' said Murdo.

'If you don't believe me, try him out. Ask him anything and he'll give you the correct answer.'

'Hey, Red Cloud, where am I from?' asked the Scot.

'Glasgow, on the great River Clyde,' replied the Memory Man and, of course, he was right.

'Right,' said Murdo, 'that was too easy and you probably recognised my accent. So here's a more difficult one. Who won the Scottish League Cup Final in 1971?'

'Partick Thistle,' said Red Cloud.

'And who did they play?' asked Murdo.

'Celtic,' Red Cloud said, without blinking.

'And the score after thirty-seven minutes?' asked Murdo.

'4–0 to Partick Thistle,' replied the Memory Man without hesitation.

'Very good, but I'll bet you $40 that you don't know who scored the fourth goal,' said Murdo.

'Jimmy Bone,' replied Red Cloud.

Flabbergasted, Murdo handed Red Cloud $40 and left the bar. On his return to Glasgow, Murdo just couldn't get Red Cloud out of his mind and decided that he must visit him again. So the following year when Murdo was on his next sales trip to America he went back to the town to visit the Memory Man. And when he walked into the bar, he saw Red Cloud in his usual corner.

Instinctively, Murdo raised his arm and greeted Red Cloud in the traditional Indian fashion: 'How!'

Memory Man squinted at the Scot, paused for a moment and then replied, 'From just outside the six-yard box.'

(2 marks)

TOTAL MARKS AVAILABLE FOR SECTION XI: 24

THE CANDIDATE'S SCORE:

APPENDIX 1

THE TEST ANSWERS

I. GENDER STUDIES

1.1   Both (i) and (ii) caused serious damage, as did the two
       illustrations below:

1.2   (i) and (ii) are correct, and the divorce was by mutual
       agreement.

1.3   (i) No, and in some parts of Scotland, including at least two
       famous golf clubs, this view is, on occasions, still voiced.

1.4   Both, of course, are correct, and another one that you may
       have considered is:

       'I started off in life with nothing and I've still got most of it left.'

1.5   Both are correct. More chauvinistic options would include:

       'My husband and I fight about sex and money. He believes that
       I charge too much.'

       'I only talk to my husband while having sex if I'm next to my
       mobile.'

1.6   All three are correct, and it is always in the sequence set down
       in the question.

1.7   Neither is correct. Both men were in fact doctors, but the
       response did cure the patient's hiccups (see also question 4.8).

1.8   (i) is correct, and two bonus marks if you noticed the weak pun on 'affair'.

1.9   Four marks if you selected three or more of the options, and see below for several others that may also strike a chord:

'Iconoclastic cross-dresser seeks woman, size 16, with DW, impeccable taste and fabulous wardrobe.'

'Fiscally conservative Aberdonian seeks woman with limited interest in shopping, dining out, foreign holidays or jewellery. Please send SAE for further details.'

'RB parasitic Paisley polecat with raffish good looks seeks new female host. The likely lady will have a limited grasp on reality.'

1.10   Obviously (ii) is correct. For a picture of Hugh, please see the illustration in 5.2.

1.11   (ii) is correct, and note that coincidentally Bill had previously been married to Hugh's wife (see 1.10 and 5.2).

1.12   All four are correct, and for two bonus marks, please answer the following:

Before going out for the day, a Scotsman locked his wife and his dog in the garage. When he returned and opened the door, who was happier to see him?

(i) The wife   ☐   (ii) The dog   ☐

The answer is (ii).

II. SCOTTISH LANGUAGE

2.1   (i) 'Yes', and here are a few more linguistic differences:

EDINBURGH	GLASGOW	EDINBURGH	GLASGOW
Toupee	Rug	Conservatory	Greenhouse
Face	Coupon	Four-by-four	Bogie
Supper	Tea	Bruise	Nukkie badge
Punishment exercise	Punny eccy		

2.2   (i) Yes, and not before time.

See below for a third new entry for the next edition:

2.3   (iii) Country music is correct, and please answer the following
       supplementary question:

       Tartan-collar Scotland has developed an irrepressible affection
       for country music. For two bonus marks, which of the following
       such songs topped Scotland's country music charts between
       1990 and 2000?

       If I Had Shot You When I Wanted To, I'd Be Out By Now   ☐

       My Wife Ran Off With My Best Friend, and I Sure Do
       Miss Him   ☐

If the Phone Don't Ring, You'll Know It's Me ☐

I'm Sick and Tired of Waking Up So Sick and Tired ☐

Answer: all of the above.

2.4 (ii) All except Edinburgh, and for two bonus marks please answer the following question:

Does the date on the taxi's number plate refer to:

(i) The Battle of Bannockburn ☐

(ii) The Battle of the Boyne ☐

The answer is (i). Anyone answering (ii) loses ten marks.

2.5 (i) Agree. And becauzz rarburirinlaw was the headhighheidyin inra polis, ra drivir goatoff wi ah wornin.

2.6 (i) Yes, and an alternative set of captions could be as follows:

2.7   Both options are correct, so one mark for each box ticked. A bonus mark if you know either of the following two 'wurds':

Frostitute: A Morningside lady of easy virtue.
Blunderstanding: The way in which the Scottish Parliament agreed to hold the Referendum.

2.8   (ii) 2007 is an acceptable answer, but strictly speaking it was closer to 2000, the date that the wee blue pill became available on the NHS.

2.9   (ii) No, and strictly speaking this is only a West Central Scotland joke.

2.10   The answer is (ii), but according to a male urban myth a woman's reaction may, on occasion, be different.

III. POLITICS AND INTERNATIONAL RELATIONS

3.1   Ironically, (i) and (ii) are both correct. Two bonus marks if you also suggested:

(i) Whozaskin or (ii) Tellyaramorra

3.2   (ii) Cynical, but, as the Referendum debate reaches fever pitch, there have been reports of similar situations where there has been a dog with even more than two arseholes.

3.3   (i) Yes is correct, but any resemblance between the left-hand-side panda and the Great Leader is purely coincidental.

3.4   (iii) Glasgow Royal Infirmary, and before Rangers' demise you could also have added Old Firm matches.

3.5   The correct answer is (ii) No. And award yourself two bonus marks if you have some sympathy for any of the views expressed below:

'Global Warming may not necessarily be the cause of England's winter floods.'
Elle Nino, Girvan

'Why was England not better prepared for the winter rains?'
Noah S. Ark & Wayne E. Days, Clydebank

'You'd think that floods were something new.'
Andy DeLuvian, Greenock

3.6   Both are urban myths, as is, 'I resemble that remark.'

3.7   (i) Yes is correct, and for two bonus marks, is this the Better Together campaign's proposed new tartan?

    (i) Yes ☐   (iii) No ☐

Answer: (ii) No, and sources close to the SNP believe any such tartan would look as follows:

3.8　(i) Yes, and for two bonus marks, please answer the following question:

If you were a masochist and Scotland voted for Independence, what would be your choice for the country's new national anthem?

(i) Swing Low, Sweet Chariot ☐

(ii) On Ilkla Moor Baht 'at ☐

(iii) Jerusalem ☐

(iv) The Eton Boating Song ☐

Answer: any one of the above would do the trick.

3.9   It's both (i) and (ii). If you've not spotted Alistair Darling, he is hiding in the middle right of the cartoon.

Unless the economy picks up, Edinburgh Zoo's cubless pandas may have to be replaced by less expensive but similar looking animals:

3.10   The first three options are correct, but it was actually Norman Conquest who asked 'Would England invade?' and not Norman D. Landings.

3.11   Both answers are correct. Two bonus marks if you knew that the pop-up book topped the bestseller list in Glasgow for six months.

3.12   (ii) is correct, and below is an illustration of said Post Tortoise:

IV. SCOTTISH MEDICINE AND SCIENCE

4.1 All four answers are correct, and the following would also be acceptable:

(i) Dodgy genes   (ii) Margaret Thatcher

4.2 (ii) 100% is correct. To further understand the Tartan Army's psyche, please read and digest the following parable:

A Tartan Army stalwart staggered back to his hotel after yet another away defeat when he chanced across a fairy who, seeing how downcast he was, granted him one wish.

The supporter gladly took up the offer and said, 'I want to live forever.'

'Sorry,' said the fairy, 'but I'm not allowed to grant wishes like that.'

'Fair enough,' said the supporter. 'I want to end my days when Scotland win the World Cup.'

'You crafty bastard!' replied the fairy.

4.3 (iii) Premature Jock Elation. Also note that this condition can also strike the Tartan Army when Saxonia go one down only to equalise and then score a late winner in Fergie Time.

4.4 All these methods are effective, but (iii), Tartan Underwear, is probably the most reliable and widely used.

4.5 (iii) The space suit, but see right for the less expensive emergency option:

© Shutterstock

4.6   All four are correct, and the Examination Board would also accept 'fossil' as an answer.

4.7   (i) Yes, and the man in the next bed also bought his socks.

4.8   (i) Yes, and for another medical question and two bonus marks:

Please rearrange the letters P-N-E-S-I to spell out the most important part of the male anatomy

The answer is spine. Please deduct four marks if you gave any other answer.

4.9   Two marks if at least three boxes have been ticked. Other acceptable answers include:

'Scots should take more exercise.'
Jim Naseum, Clydebank

'After drinking Saxon beer, I feel ill. What's in it?'
Nat S. Piss, Anstruther

'While camping in Skye I developed a very itchy rash. What could be causing this?'
Midge E. Bytes, Mallaig

'Contrary to mainstream medical opinion, I think that Scots should eat more fried food.'
Crispin Dry, Thurso

4.10   Both (i) and (ii) are correct. While on the subject of sad but amusing stories, and for two bonus marks, is the following tale:

(i) Sad ☐   (ii) Amusing ☐

'The wife's been missing for over a week now and the police asked me to prepare for the worst, so I've been down to Oxfam to get all her clothes back.'

Answer: (ii) (very) amusing.

4.11   (iii) Large.

V. SOCIOLOGY

5.1 (i) Absolutely, and young Murray also has a very good sense of timing.

5.2 (ii) Too little too late, and two bonus marks if you knew that there are many more Shades of Grey than Great Scottish Goals.

5.3 The answers are interchangeable, and two bonus marks if you can answer the following correctly:

You are driving down the A9 in your sports car on a wild, stormy night and you see three people waiting for a bus:

(i) An old lady who looks as if she is on her last legs ☐

(ii) An old friend ☐

(iii) The perfect partner you have been dreaming about ☐

Knowing that there was only room for one passenger in your car, which one of the three would you pick up?
The ethically correct answer is to give the car keys to the old friend and have him/her take the old lady to the hospital. You would stay behind and wait for the bus with the partner of your dreams. However, the correct 'Scottish' answer is to run the old lady over to put her out of her misery, make out with the perfect partner on the bonnet of the car and then drive off with the old friend for a few beers.

5.4 Paradoxically, (i) and (ii) are both correct.

5.5 (ii) Frugal, and they also carefully peeled the paint off all the doors and surrounds.

5.6 (i) Yes, and see below for the proposed design for the next generation of Strathclyde Police helicopters:

5.7 Knowing Tam, it would be both (i) and (ii).

5.8 (i) Yes, and 'there's no point, they'll find us eventually' is a very common response in Scotland and usually covers a multitude of situations involving either family issues or 'the authorities'.

5.9 (ii) No, it is not possible to further enhance a Scotsman's reputation for strength and masculinity.

And for no extra marks, do you agree with the answer to the following related question?

Q. How would you kill a circus?
A. Go for the juggler.

5.10 (ii) The Scot. On a related point, were you aware that if you counted all the pies bought at Scottish football matches over a weekend, the chances would be that you were autistic?

VI. MODERN STUDIES

6.1   Obviously (iv), lamb rogan josh.

6.2   (iv) Nitro, and rumour has it that eating Fifi in the final round clinched the title for him.

6.3   (i) True, and please see below for the most recent 'retro' design proposal for the next generation of number 20 buses:

6.4   All four are popular both in and beyond Paisley. Give yourself two marks if you ticked at least two from the list. Other acceptable Paisley proverbs are:

'Policemen's shoes never squeak.'
'Never trust the window cleaner.'
'Better late than pregnant.'

6.5 All four are correct, and two bonus marks if you can answer the following question:

Although the photograph below will certainly keep kids away from the hearth, does it also provide a compelling argument against Independence?

(i) Yes ☐   (ii) No ☐

The answer is most definitely (i) yes.

6.6 (iii) is correct, but only if you can afford the 'lecky'.

6.7 (i) Zero, and on that night some 100 decoys were deployed throughout Scotland. On Saturdays that figure can rise to over 600.

6.8 (i) and (ii) are both correct, and the Street Talk comment below would also be acceptable:

'The police should adopt a zero tolerance approach towards teenagers.'
Harrison Chavs-Daily, Dunblane

6.9 (i) is correct. If you answered (ii) then deduct ten marks, as there is obviously no need for such facilities in Scotland.

6.10 (ii) No. In fact, the winner was:

'My girlfriend thinks that I'm a stalker. Well, she's not exactly my girlfriend yet.'

6.11 (i) by Nick Helm is correct, and here are three others from that year's shortlist:

'Once I'd hired the car, the drive-thru McDonald's was more expensive than I thought.'

'I was playing chess with a friend and he said, "Let's make this more interesting." So we stopped playing chess.'

'My friend died doing what he loved most . . . heroin.'

VII. PHILOSOPHY AND THEOLOGY

7.1 (i) is correct, but only just.

7.2 Many evolutionary biologists believe that this is the reason:

7.3   (i) Absolutely is correct, and for two bonus marks here is another question in a similar vein:

Is 'bingo' a witty euphemism?

Yes   Yes

A girl from Dumbarton left home to find fame and fortune in London. She came home for a visit some six months later but to the surprise of her mother she arrived in a limo and wearing a full-length mink coat.

'Heather,' said her mother, 'that's a lovely fur coat you're wearin', but how can you afford it?'

Heather replied, 'I won it at the bingo, Mum, they have wonderful prizes in London.'

When the weekend was over, Heather returned to the bright lights, but she came back to visit again a few months later. This time she was wearing a beautiful gold watch and a matching diamond ring.

The usual exchange with mum followed, with Heather explaining that she 'won it at the bingo!'.

After the visit Heather returned to the capital, but a few months later she was back in Dumbarton again. This time she was sporting a stunning diamond necklace with a matching bracelet and earrings. She also had a gift of £1,000 for her mother and explained that she won it all at the bingo. Then she asked her mum to run a bath, as she needed to freshen up after her journey.

Her mum drew the bath while Heather unpacked, but when Heather saw that there was only a quarter-inch of water in the bath, she was a little peeved at her mum's frugality and asked, 'Mum, why is there only a quarter of an inch of water in the bath?'

'Well, my darling,' replied her mum, 'we don't want your bingo card getting wet now, do we?'

Answer: (i) Yes.

7.4

$$\left(\int \begin{array}{c} y=+\sqrt{P} \quad (a^2-b^2)+2abi \quad x\times(a+ib) \\ \left(\dfrac{4x\,dx=1m}{+g\,(\pi(2+x))}\right)=\left\{\dfrac{O}{O}\right\}=\begin{array}{c}\pi \\ \lim_{x=0}\end{array} \\ \sum \underbrace{\wedge\wedge\wedge\wedge} \quad (E\times B)\to E=\frac{1}{2}\hbar k/m \\ \begin{array}{c}\mathcal{L}=Y \\ \#=X \\ \hbar=+\end{array}\left(1-\dfrac{2k}{2k+1}\right)=X^2 \quad =(B=(P-1)) \\ 0<n^2+S^2<P \end{array}\right)$$

7.5   (ii) Absolutely not, unless it was a Sunday in the Outer Hebrides.

7.6   None of the above. The correct answer is Strathclyde Police.

7.7   None of the above. The answer is 4 x 109, as the photograph below illustrates:

© Superstock

7.8   It's four! This is the test's disguised 'ethics and values' question, so deduct six marks if you ticked either of the options on offer.

VIII. SCOTTISH HISTORY, CULTURE AND THE ARTS

8.1   Of course the answer is (i) William Wallace. And below is a reproduction of one of the most famous scenes from the film Braveherd, an homage to the life of William Wallace. It depicts the moment when William Wallace and a few Highland cattle routed the Saxons:

8.2   Both (i) and (ii) were voted top equal in a recent poll, along with Maradona.

8.3   All options are correct, and henceforth it should be known as the Scottish Empire.

8.4   (iv) *Gregory's Girl*, and close on its heels are *Braveherd* (see also 8.1) and *Brigadoon*.

8.5   All four were famous Scottish ballet dancers.

8.6   (i) and (ii) are both wrong. The real saying is: 'See Wishaw and die.'

8.7   All three are correct, and two bonus marks if you also suggested:

Six foot two, eyes of blue
Big Jim Holton's after you.

8.8 (i) Absolutely. History tells us that he hit her on the head with a shovel and so hostilities broke out once more and continue to this day.

8.9 None of the above. Fifty Shades Of Tartan is the title of the top-selling guide book to the Royal Mile.

IX. BUSINESS AND BANKING

9.1 (i) and (ii) are both correct: both were obviously guilty, as were the usual suspects, Jimmy Hill and John Terry.

9.2 All three are correct, as are the following:

'Surely no banker will get into heaven now?'
Pearl E. Gates, North Berwick

'We should bring back the birch for bankers and their like.'
Corporal Punishment, Eve N. Waterboarding, Balerno

'What would have happened if the government had not bailed out the banks?'
Anne Archy, Blackhill

9.3 Sadly, the answer is (i) yes.

And for two bonus marks, what is the difference between the New Towns of Livingston and Edinburgh?

(i)   Fifteen miles
(ii) Two hundred years
(iii) The local accent
(iv) The unemployment rate

Answer: all four are correct.

9.4   All three are correct, and the following would also be acceptable:

'How did Goodwin avoid going to jail?'
Hugh Deaney, Falkirk

'Surely it is obvious who was responsible for the collapse of RBS.'
Fred Didit, Andy Ranaway, Comiston

9.5   The correct answer is, in fact, 21.40 on 18th September 2014.

9.6   (ii) is correct. Note that both supermarket trolleys and the non-executive directors of banks are often found miles away from where they should be and hence once again absent without leave.

9.7   (ii) 100%, and note that by the looks of it ET should have worn some Factor 60 to protect himself from Edinburgh's fierce summer sun.

9.8   (i) Instinctively, particularly as 'nosey wee Weegies' have very few friends to phone.

And for two bonus marks, what do you call a Scottish sheep with no head or legs?

(i) Lamb chops ☐   (ii) A cloud ☐

Answer: technically (i) lamb chops, but cloud is more amusing.

9.9   All are true, as is the following:

'We need more immigrants as soon as possible.'
Kitty Exhausted, Owen Billions, Dunkeld

9.10 (ii) It's even more worser. Note that during the recession the Tooth Fairy has faced many attempts from people prepared to use deception for monetary gain. As a result, many teeth have been returned along with the standard letter reproduced below.

For two bonus marks, please tick which improprieties you may have been guilty of:

Dear Customer

Thank you for leaving your tooth/teeth under the pillow last night. While we make every attempt to leave a monetary reward in return for teeth, on this occasion we were unable to process your request for one or more of the following reason(s):

(i)   This is an adult's tooth.   ☐

(ii) Chicken bones are not acceptable.   ☐

(iii) This tooth had previously been redeemed for cash.   ☐

(iv) You never ever believed in the Tooth Fairy.   ☐

(v) We are unable to process more than ten teeth per visit.   ☐

X. APPLIED MATHEMATICS

10.1   (ii) is correct. Before sentencing, the judge overheard Dobbie say the following to Deeks:

'I saw a poor old lady fall over on the ice today! At least I presume she was poor – she only had £1.20 in her purse.'

10.2   If the game is at Celtic Park, the answer is (iv) 'never', and if it is at Ibrox, the answer is (iii) 'constantly'.

10.3   Neither answer is correct: Dixie never sobered up.

10.4 There is no correct answer. Although at first glance the answer may seem to be '9', the correct answer for the row, this does fit with the answer for the column, which is '3'. The reason is that, out of devilment, the numbers in rows three and four are the same.

Award yourself two bonus marks if you can complete the 'Super Fiendish' Senga Sudoku puzzle reproduced below:

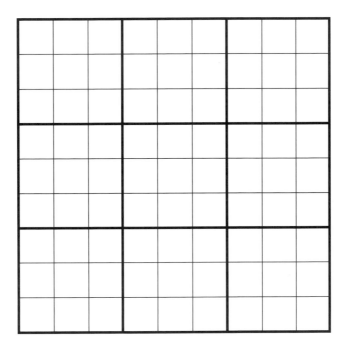

10.5 (ii) 0%. The only 100% answer would have been Gerard Butler.

10.6 (ii) No, there's a mistake in the seventh line.

10.7 (iii) Banjo got the job, and by way of background, the councillor was his uncle and Tam his nephew.

10.8 He soon discovered that his keys were missing but could not have retraced his steps to the pub even if he so wished. The whole procedure, however, did take the entire weekend.

XI. SCOTTISH SPORTS STUDIES

11.1 (iv) Scotland, but forget about the 'top ten' bit.

11.2 (ii) Yes, but unfortunately for Rangers Superman went to St Pius.

11.3 (i) and (ii) are correct and were said by, respectively, the less-than-legendary Sam Leitch and a 'Scottish TV presenter'.

For two bonus marks, can you spot another Saxon blunder from the two quoted below?

'With news of Scotland's 0–0 victory over Holland . . .'

'We'll have more football later. Meanwhile, here are the highlights from the Scottish Cup final.'

The answer is obviously the second one: this was Gary Newbon. The first quote is probably apocryphal, as no one is prepared to claim ownership.

11.4 (i) Yes, and this set of circumstances is remarkably common at Old Firm matches.

11.5 (ii), and never underestimate anyone called Jake.

11.6 (ii) was as official as it gets. Other unofficial responses include:

'Laugh? Ah nearly passed ma fags round.'

'But now ray huvva majik goal-line vidjo playback.'

11.7 (i) Yes, and predictably this fate is only reserved for Tom Daley, the Saxonian diver and favourite for the gold medal.

11.8 (ii) and (iv) are the acceptable answers. And note that revisionist Scottish historians now teach that the embarrassing 3–9 and 1–5 scores were reversed on appeal.

11.9 The correct answer is (ii) the second, when out on the street: Andy Goram. Neither Frank Haffey nor Stuart Kennedy would have been acceptable answers.

11.10 (i) Alain Baxter. Robbed of a slalom medal at Salt Lake City Olympics, Alain recently received a special Braveheart award for dying his hair blue and in the shape of the Saltire Cross during the said Olympic event. The campaign to 'return' his Olympic medal is ongoing. Eddie the Eagle's only post-Olympic initiative was a vainglorious attempt to exempt ski jumpers from paying taxes.

11.11 Both answers are acceptable. The 'contact sport' pictured below would also have been considered correct:

11.12 (ii) No. Red Cloud was wrong, as Jimmy Bone was just inside the six-yard box.

FINAL SCORES

Section	Marks Available	Candidate's Score	Per cent Scored
I. Gender Studies	26		
II. Scottish Language	22		
III. Politics and International Relations	26		
IV. Scottish Medicine and Science	24		
V. Sociology	22		
VI. Modern Studies	26		
VII. Philosophy and Theology	22		
VIII. Scottish History, Culture and the Arts	22		
IX. Business and Banking	24		
X. Applied Mathematics	22		
XI. Scottish Sports Studies	24		
Bonus Marks Available in the Answers	40		
TOTAL	300		

Signed by Candidate:	
Signed by Examiner:	
Witness:	
Date:	

WHAT YOUR SCORES MEAN

0–74 marks:

About as Scottish as Morris Dancing

A serious fail. Have you ever considered emigrating?

75–149 marks:

Berwick-on-Tweed

Just a little 'south of the border'. Try again in the next Referendum

150–224 marks:

A Jock Tamson's Bairn

It is recommended that you exercise your vote, subject to the requirement of having scored above 80% in both the Gender and Modern Studies sections

225–300 marks:

Indeed a Lad or Lass o' Pairts

Vote early and vote often

APPENDIX 2

FREQUENTLY ASKED
QUESTIONS

Q	*Can Scotland keep the pound?*
A	Mibbi aye, mibbi naw.

Q	*Will Scotland still be in the EU?*
A	Mibbi aye, mibbi naw.

Q	*My wife is a Saxon. Will she be entitled to a Scottish passport?*
A	Naw.

Q	*Is our oil running out?*
A	Aye.

Q	*If Scotland becomes independent, will Berwick Rangers still be allowed to play in the Scottish Football League?*
A	Naw.

Q	*Can we still go abroad on our holidays?*
A	Aye, but only until the oil runs out.

Q	*If the Referendum vote is 'Against', will the Bank of England be renamed?*
A	Uryi stuppit?

A NATION IN TURMOIL: SOME VIEWS ON THE REFERENDUM

Independence will set Scotland back centuries. *Hunter Gatherer*

Scotland will narrowly vote to leave the UK. *Nat S. Whisker*

A vote for Independence will end badly. *Helen Damnation*

The Referendum is turning into a witch-hunt. *Hugh N. Cry*

What will employment prospects be in an independent Scotland?
U.B. Forty

Despite its diminutive size, Scotland should still go it alone.
David N. Goliath

The politicians on both sides are just spinning us a yarn.
Pat R. Merchants

A vote for Independence means that affluent Scots will all move to
London. *Iona Ferrari*

This Referendum business will end in tears. *Mark Mywords*

If Independence doesn't work, can we change our minds? *U. Turn*